The Ultimate Guide to
THE CONMEBOL
COPA AMÉRICA
2024

Journey through South America's Premier Football
Tournament and Witness the Triumphs, Drama,
and Glory of the Continent's Finest

Gina Salomon

CONTENTS

Introduction to the Copa America

Copa America, also referred to as the South American Football Championship, is the top international football competition in South America. Having been established in 1916, it has the distinction of being the oldest international continental football tournament, having existed even before the FIFA World Cup. The rich footballing tradition and passionate fan culture of South America are on display in this storied competition, which has become a symbol of excellence in the international footballing community.

The historical beginnings of the Copa America can be traced back to the early 20th century, at a time when football was experiencing a surge in popularity throughout South American countries. The South American Football Confederation (CONMEBOL) was established in 1916, which was the beginning of the establishment of regional tournaments from that point on. The first ever Copa America was played in Argentina, and the four countries who took part in the competition were Uruguay, Brazil, Chile, and Argentina. Since that time, the event has become more prestigious and significant, which has resulted in it being a treasured tradition for football fans all around the globe.

Throughout its history, the Copa America has undergone a process of evolution to suit the shifting dynamics that have occurred within the world of football. The tournament format has been subjected to several revisions, including increases in the number of teams who are playing and modifications to the organization of the competition. While originally contested by just a few South American countries, Copa America currently involves teams from both CONMEBOL and invited visitors from other confederations, providing a global flavor to the competition.

Structure and Competition Structure: Copa America normally follows a structure consisting of a group stage followed by elimination rounds, ending in the final match to decide the winner. The number of participating teams and the tournament format may change from edition to edition, based on variables like hosting agreements and organizational decisions by CONMEBOL. The tournament is recognized for its exciting and intensely fought encounters, typically highlighting the flair, ability, and competitive spirit of South American football.

The importance of Copa America cannot be overstated, not just in South America but also on an international scale. Its legacy is both significant and enduring. It provides a forum for showing the great skill and footballing expertise of South American countries while also developing brotherhood and mutual respect among competing teams. The tournament has produced innumerable spectacular moments, iconic performances, and famous players who have left an indelible stamp on the history of football.

Beyond the sphere of athletics, Copa America is firmly rooted in the cultural fabric of South America. It crosses boundaries and unites individuals from varied origins under a shared love for football. The tournament's exciting atmosphere, exuberant celebrations, and strong support from supporters make a unique experience for players and viewers alike. Copa America serves as a celebration of South American culture, tradition, and mutual passion for the beautiful game.

As the oldest international continental football tournament, Copa America epitomizes the spirit of competitiveness, friendship, and excellence. It stands as a testimony to the long history of South American football and continues to inspire generations of players and spectators throughout the globe. With each edition, Copa America reinforces its reputation as a top event in the global football calendar, capturing fans with its drama, emotion, and absolute talent on the field.

Overview of the Copa America 2024

Copa America 2024 promises to be a fantastic demonstration of footballing skill, passion, and competitiveness when South America's top teams assemble to vie for continental supremacy. As one of the most prominent competitions in international football, the Copa America retains a particular place in the hearts of supporters worldwide.

Here's what to anticipate from year's edition:

Host Nation and Venues: The host nation of Copa America 2024 will serve as the bright background for the tournament's festivities. With a long football legacy and an ardent fan base, the host country will welcome teams and fans from around South America and beyond. State-of-the-art stadiums and renowned locations will provide the setting for exciting matches and memorable moments.

Participating Teams: Copa America 2024 will include a variety of teams showcasing the finest of South American football. Traditional powerhouses like Brazil, Argentina, Uruguay, and Chile will be among the favorites to take the title, but new competitors will attempt to make their impact on the event. The tournament promises to be closely fought, with every side aiming for dominance in the continental arena.

Tournament Structure: The structure of the Copa America 2024 will follow the established pattern of group stages and knockout rounds. Teams will be placed into groups, where they will play against each other in a round-robin manner. The best teams from each group will proceed to the knockout round, when single-elimination matches will decide the final winner. The tournament structure promises big stakes and strong competition from start to end.

Key Players and Storylines: The Copa America 2024 will feature some of the world's finest gifted players, each ready to make their imprint on the event. From established greats to developing prospects, athletes will have the chance to flourish on the continental stage and engrave their names into football legacy. Compelling narratives, rivalries, and drama are guaranteed to engage viewers throughout the tournament.

Expectations and Predictions: As anticipation develops for Copa America 2024, fans and commentators alike will speculate on probable scenarios and favorites for the championship. Traditional powerhouses will face fierce competition from up-and-coming teams, bringing an element of unpredictability to the event. Golden Boot contenders, outstanding performances, and underdog tales will add to the excitement and intrigue of Copa America 2024.

Global Impact and Legacy: Copa America 2024 will transcend boundaries and fascinate spectators across the globe, showing the international appeal of football and the passion of South American supporters. The tournament's impact will remain long beyond the final whistle, leaving an indelible effect on the sport and motivating future generations of players and spectators.

Copa America 2024 aims to be a celebration of footballing brilliance, togetherness, and enthusiasm. With exciting matches, spectacular moments, and a display of talent from around South America, the tournament will grab the imagination of spectators and reassert its place as one of the best events in world football. As teams prepare to vie for triumph, the scene is prepared for a memorable adventure at Copa America 2024.

History of the Copa America

Copa America remains a monument to the great legacy, passion, and quality of South American football. Since its start in

1916, the competition has developed into one of the most renowned and keenly awaited events on the football calendar.

A tour through the history of Copa America, chronicling its beginnings, progress, and lasting legacy:

Founding Years (1916–1929): Copa America was founded out of a desire to display the developing football potential of South America. The first event was held in 1916 in Argentina, with the home country emerging as the first winners. Initially named the "South American Championship," the event included only four teams: *Argentina, Brazil, Chile, and Uruguay.* Over the following decade, Copa America rose in popularity and importance, gaining growing attention from football lovers across the continent.

Expansion and Consolidation (1930s–1950s): The 1930s saw Copa America increase both in terms of participant clubs and geographical reach. New countries like Peru, Paraguay, and Bolivia entered the competition, giving depth and variety to the event. The 1940s and 1950s featured fierce rivalry and spectacular encounters, with Uruguay and Argentina establishing themselves as dominating powers in South American football. Iconic players such as Jose Nasazzi, Hector Scarone, and Alfredo Di Stefano made an everlasting impression on the event during this period.

Golden Era and Global Recognition (1960s–1980s): The 1960s were an era of transformation and innovation for Copa America. The tournament expanded to include additional teams, with CONMEBOL nations fighting for continental dominance.

Brazil emerged as a dominating force, exhibiting the mesmerizing abilities of players like Pele, Garrincha, and Zico. The 1970s and 1980s saw the globalization of Copa America, with matches broadcast to audiences throughout the globe. The tournament's prestige skyrocketed, solidifying its standing as a premier event in world football.

Contemporary Age and Continued Success (1990s—Present): In the contemporary age, Copa America has continued to attract spectators with its combination of tradition, passion, and talent. The competition has responded to shifting dynamics within the football scene, bringing new forms and innovations to improve the fan experience. Nations like Colombia, Chile, and Ecuador have emerged as serious rivals, challenging the old powerhouses for dominance in the continental arena. The tournament's persistent popularity and worldwide reach have maintained its status as one of the most prominent events in international football.

Influence & Impact: Copa America's influence stretches well beyond the sphere of athletics, defining the cultural character of South America and inspiring generations of players and spectators. The tournament has produced classic moments, renowned players, and spectacular matches that have left an everlasting stamp on the history of football. From the Maracanazo to the Miracle of Santiago, Copa America has provided the venue for glory, sadness, and everything in between. As the tournament continues to adapt and flourish, its heritage remains a monument to the lasting power of this wonderful game.

Copa America serves as a symbol of greatness, passion, and solidarity in South American football. From its modest origins in 1916 to its stature as a worldwide spectacle in the 21st century, the tournament has remained faithful to its traditions while embracing innovation and advancement. As supporters anxiously anticipate each edition of Copa America, they do so with a feeling of respect for the tournament's rich past and a hopeful optimism for the future of football on the continent.

Format & Structure of Copa America 2024

Copa America 2024 will have an intriguing format and structure meant to showcase the finest of South American football skills while giving spectators thrilling matches and memorable moments.

Group Stage: The competition will commence with the group stage, when the competing teams will be placed into groups, normally consisting of four teams each. The actual number of groups and teams per group may change based on the overall number of participating countries. Teams will participate in a round-robin style, playing against each other once. Points will be given for victories, draws, and defeats, with the top teams from each group proceeding to the knockout round.

Knockout Stage: Following the group stage, the competition will transfer into the knockout round, often known as the knockout rounds or elimination rounds. The knockout stage will comprise single-elimination matches, where the winner goes to the next round and the loser is removed from the tournament. The elimination stage will comprise matches such as the quarter-finals, semi-finals, and the highly anticipated final match to decide the winner of Copa America 2024.

Final Match: The climax of Copa America 2024 will be the final match, where the two greatest teams from the knockout stage will square off for continental supremacy. The final match will be staged in a notable site, often a recognized stadium within the host nation. It will be an exhibition of ability, tenacity, and emotion as the finalists vie for the coveted Copa America trophy and the title of champions of South America.

Tiebreakers and Passage Criteria: In the case of teams completing the group stage with identical points, tiebreakers will be utilized to determine the standings and passage to the knockout round. Tiebreakers may include goal difference, goals scored, head-to-head results, and other factors stated by the tournament rules. The criteria for progression and tiebreakers will be defined in full in the official Copa America 2024 rules.

Additional Elements: In addition to the group stage and knockout stage, Copa America 2024 may incorporate more elements and innovations to improve the tournament experience. This might include special prizes for exceptional performances, fan interaction efforts, cultural events, and more. The event organizers will endeavor to provide a memorable and engaging experience for players, spectators, and stakeholders alike.

The concept and organization of Copa America 2024 are intended to bring excitement, drama, and world-class football to fans throughout the globe. With an exciting group stage, dramatic knockout rounds, and a magnificent final match, the event promises to be a celebration of the beautiful game and the rich footballing history of South America. As nations prepare to fight for continental supremacy, expectations are high for what promises to be a spectacular edition of Copa America.

Chapter 1: HOST COUNTRY AND VENUES

Copa America 2024 will unfold against the background of a lively host nation, selected to embrace the essence of South American football and give a memorable setting for the event. From famous stadiums steeped in footballing history to contemporary grounds built to showcase the beautiful game, the host country will welcome teams and supporters with open arms. Each arena will throb with the energy of dedicated fans, producing an exciting atmosphere that will reverberate throughout the tournament. As the action unfolds on the field, the host nation and its venues will serve as important characters in the drama of Copa America 2024, leaving an unforgettable impression on players and fans alike.

Host Country of the Copa America 2024

The selection of the United States of America as the host nation for Copa America 2024 marks a new chapter in the tournament's historic history. Renowned for its enthusiasm for sports and vibrant cultures, the United States promises to offer an unrivaled venue for the celebration of South American football greatness. As the host country, the United States will have a vital role in crafting the tournament experience for players, spectators, and stakeholders alike.

One of the key advantages of the United States as a host nation is its world-class infrastructure. From iconic stadiums to cutting-edge transportation networks, the country is well-equipped to support a major international event. These venues will provide the perfect backdrop for exciting matches and unforgettable moments in the game.

As a nation known for its diversity, the United States embodies the spirit of inclusion that is at the heart of football. The competition will bring together fans from all walks of life, united by their love for the beautiful game. The host cities will be buzzing with excitement as fans come together to celebrate the spirit of football.

Copa America 2024 is poised to leave a lasting legacy on American soccer. By showcasing the beautiful game to a wide audience, the event will inspire a new generation of players and fans, furthering the development of soccer at all levels. The exposure gained by hosting Copa America will also solidify the United States' position as a destination for international sporting events.

The successful staging of Copa America 2024 will be a testament to the collaborative efforts of various stakeholders. Through strategic partnerships and meticulous planning, these groups will work together to ensure the tournament's smooth execution. By combining their resources and expertise, they will deliver an exceptional experience for participants and spectators alike.

Copa America 2024 presents a unique opportunity to promote football culture in the United States and beyond. Through various initiatives, the event will engage fans of all ages and backgrounds, fostering a deeper appreciation for the sport and its values. By promoting inclusion, fair play, and teamwork, Copa America will leave a positive mark on society, encouraging people to embrace the spirit of football on and off the field.

Venues and Stadiums

Below is a list of the stadiums, locations, locations, and capacity for the tournament:

Stadium	Venue	Capacity
AT&T Stadium	Arlington, Texas	80,000
Mercedes-Benz Stadium	Atlanta, Georgia	71,000
Q2 Stadium	Austin, Texas	20,738
Bank of America Stadium	Charlotte, North Carolina	74,867
MetLife Stadium	East Rutherford, New Jersey	82,566

NRG Stadium	Houston, Texas	72,220
SoFi Stadium	Inglewood, California	70,240
Levi's Stadium	Santa Clara, California	68,500
State Farm Stadium	Glendale, Arizona	63,400
Allegiant Stadium	Las Vegas, Nevada	61,000
GEHA Field at Arrowhead Stadium	Kansas City, Missouri	76,416
Children's Mercy Park	Kansas City, Kansas	18,467
Hard Rock Stadium	Miami Gardens, Florida	64,767
Inter & Co Stadium	Orlando, Florida	25,500)

This will be just the second time the Copa América has been staged outside of South America since the original competition in 1916.

Chapter 2: PARTICIPATING TEAMS

The Copa America 2024 will feature a variety of teams showcasing the finest of South American football skills. From old powerhouses to budding challengers, each competing team brings its distinct style and capabilities to the event. With a long tradition of strong competition and spectacular performances, Copa America aims to display the talent, passion, and friendship that characterize the sport. As supporters anxiously await the event, they do so with enthusiasm and expectation, ready to see which teams will rise to the occasion and make their imprint on the continental stage. With every match likely to bring thrills, drama, and moments of genius, Copa America 2024 promises to be a celebration of footballing greatness and a monument to the continuing fascination of the beautiful game.

Copa América is expanding in 2024, with six teams from North America joining the normal 10 countries from South America that participate in the continental tournament. The format mimics the Copa América Centenario in 2016, the only prior occasion the competition was hosted outside of South America.

List of the teams that qualified for Copa America 2024:

CONMEBOL
Argentina(holders)
Bolivia
Brazil
Chile
Colombia
Ecuador
Paraguay
Peru
Uruguay
Venezuela

CONCACAF
Panama
USA
Jamaica
Mexico
Canada
Costa Rica

A total of 16 teams will play in the 2024 Copa America (10 from CONMEBOL and six from CONCACAF), and the group stage will include four groups of four teams each.

10 CONMEBOL sides have earned automatic qualifying slots for the tournament, with four from CONCACAF, with the last two CONCACAF spots determined in the March 2024 playoffs.

Canada overcame Trinidad and Tobago, while Costa Rica edged out Honduras in a one-leg playoff match, which confirmed the final 16.

Teams to Watch Out For

As Copa America 2024 approaches, many teams stand out as ones to watch for their potential to have a huge influence on the event. Traditional powerhouses like Brazil and Argentina are regular challengers, possessing tough teams and a long history of success in South American football. Uruguay, with its illustrious background and persistent competitive spirit, is another squad that attracts attention.

Chile and Colombia have frequently fared well in previous editions of Copa America, demonstrating excellent play and tactical brilliance. Ecuador and Peru, although generally regarded as underdogs, can surprise with their dynamic playing styles and growing talent.

Furthermore, the host country, the United States, has its degree of intrigue as it strives to make an impact on the world arena. With a strong fan base and a rising interest in soccer, the United States has the chance to create a mark on Copa America 2024.

These teams offer a mix of proven contenders and emerging stars, each primed to provide excitement and drama to the tournament. As The Copa the Copa America unfolds, all eyes will be on these teams as they battle for success on the continental stage.

Dark Horses of the Tournament

In the exhilarating world of football competitions like Copa America, there's always a feeling of anticipation for the underdog teams—the dark horses—who can surprise, defy expectations and make an everlasting impact on the sport. As Copa America 2024 approaches, numerous sides sit in the shadows, ready to emerge as surprising contenders and threaten the established order of South American football.

Ecuador, despite being frequently overshadowed by its more prominent neighbors, features a team overflowing with skill and promise. With a combination of seasoned veterans and intriguing new possibilities, Ecuador has the chance to disrupt the balance of power in Copa America 2024. Known for their offensive flair and high-tempo style of play, they might prove to be a strong force in the European arena.

Paraguay's history in Copa America is distinguished by moments of victory and tenacity, giving them a squad to watch in the 2018 tournament. Despite suffering struggles in recent years, Paraguay maintains a squad of quality players capable of turning heads and producing shocks. With a tactically adept approach and a never-say-die spirit, La Albirroja might surprise many and surpass expectations in Copa America 2024.

Venezuela may not have a legendary past in Copa America, but they have progressed in previous editions of the event, signaling their potential as dark horses in Copa America 2024. Blessed with a generation of bright young players and nurtured by good coaching, La Vinotinto might be primed for a breakthrough performance. With a combination of defensive stability and offensive flare, Venezuela has the skills to make a long run and create issues for more experienced sides.

As the host country, the United States wears the weight of expectation on its shoulders. However, with the development of soccer's popularity in the nation and an increasingly competitive local league, the United States might emerge as a dark horse in Copa America 2024. With a combination of seasoned veterans and developing stars, the USMNT can surprise onlookers and make a statement on the world scene.

Colombia may not be regarded as a classic dark horse, considering its great football background and prior wins in Copa America. However, recent performances have left some questioning the Los Cafeteros' capacity to fight for the crown. With a revitalized sense of purpose and a determination to retake its position among South America's best, Colombia might surprise many and surpass expectations in Copa America 2024. Led by seasoned leaders and boosted by developing stars, Colombia has the skill and resolve to make a deep run in the tournament.

Although the spotlight may shine brightest on the perennial favorites in Copa America 2024, the dark horses of the tournament lie in the shadows, ready to grab their time and make an unforgettable impact on the game. Whether it's Ecuador's offensive flair, Paraguay's perseverance, Venezuela's young enthusiasm, the United States' developing prowess, or Colombia's rebirth, these teams represent the spirit of unpredictability and excitement that characterizes football's most spectacular moments. As the competition progresses, viewers may anticipate shocks, upsets, and spectacular performances from these dark horses as they attempt to carve their names into Copa America legend.

Chapter 3: TOURNAMENT SCHEDULE

Copa America 2024 offers a compelling tournament program packed with exciting matches, dramatic moments, and outstanding performances. As the competing clubs continue on their quest for continental glory, spectators can look forward to a vibrant and action-packed tournament that will display the finest of South American football skills. With each match prepared to bring excitement and tension, the tournament schedule will unfold like a compelling novel, with twists and turns that will have viewers on the tip of their seats.

From the fierce fights of the group stage to the high-stakes drama of the knockout stages, Copa America 2024 will fascinate spectators across the globe and make a lasting mark on the football scene. As the competition unfolds, suspense will rise till the final match, when the best teams will meet in a struggle for dominance. With the tournament schedule planned to maximize excitement and enjoyment, Copa America 2024 promises to be an outstanding celebration of the beautiful game.

Group Stage Fixtures

The groups for the 48th edition of the world's oldest and most exciting national teams tournament were defined on Thursday, December 7th.

Sixteen national teams — ten from CONMEBOL and six from CONCACAF as guests — will seek glory from June 20, in the CONMEBOL Copa América 2024.

Group stage: June 21 to July 3

Group A	Group B	Group C	Group D
Argentina	Mexico	USA	Brazil
Peru	Ecuador	Uruguay	Colombia
Chile	Jamaica	Panama	Paraguay
Canada	Venezuela	Bolivia	Costa Rica

GROUP STAGE · MATCHDAY 1 of 3

TIME*	TEAM	STADIUM
Friday 21 June		
01:00	Argentina vs Canada	Mercedes-Benz Stadium
Saturday 22 June		
01:00	Peru vs Chile	AT&T Stadium
23:00	Ecuador vs Venezuela	Levi's Stadium
Sunday 23 June		
02:00	Mexico vs Jamaica	NRG Stadium
23:00	USA vs Bolivia	AT&T Stadium
Monday 24 June		
02:00	Uruguay vs Panama	Hard Rock Stadium
23:00	Colombia vs Paraguay	NRG Stadium
Tuesday 25 June		
02:00	Brazil vs Costa Rica	SoFi Stadium

GROUP STAGE · MATCHDAY 2 of 3

Tuesday 25 June		
23:00	Peru vs Canada	Children's Mercy Park
Wednesday 26 June		
02:00	Chile vs Argentina	MetLife Stadium
23:00	Ecuador vs Jamaica	Allegiant Stadium
Thursday 27 June		
02:00	Venezuela vs México	SoFi Stadium
23:00	Panama vs USA	Mercedes-Benz Stadium
Friday 28 June		
02:00	Uruguay vs Bolivia	MetLife Stadium
23:00	Colombia vs Costa Rica	State Farm Stadium
Saturday 29 June		
02:00	Paraguay vs Brazil	Allegiant Stadium

GROUP STAGE · MATCHDAY 3 of 3

Sunday 30 June		
01:00	Argentina vs Peru	Hard Rock Stadium
01:00	Canada vs Chile	Exploria Stadium
Monday 01 July		
01:00	Mexico vs Ecuador	State Farm Stadium
01:00	Jamaica vs Venezuela	Q2 Stadium
Tuesday 02 July		
02:00	Bolivia vs Panama	Exploria Stadium
02:00	USA vs Uruguay	Arrowhead Stadium
Wednesday 03 July		
02:00	Brazil vs Colombia	Levi's Stadium
02:00	Costa Rica vs Paraguay	Q2 Stadium

QUARTER FINALS

Friday 05 July		
02:00	TBD*	NRG Stadium
Saturday 06 July		
02:00	TBD	AT&T Stadium
23:00	TBD	State Farm Stadium
Sunday 07 July		
02:00	TBD	Allegiant Stadium

SEMI FINALS

Wednesday 10 July		
01:00	TBD	MetLife Stadium
Thursday 11 July		
01:00	TBD	Bank of America Stadium

3RD PLACE

Sunday 14 July		
01:00	TBD	Bank of America Stadium

FINAL

Monday 15 July		
01:00	TBD	Hard Rock Stadium

* Time zone and dates are in UTC +01:00 time zone; make sure you convert each timing to your desired time zone.

* TBD means To Be Decided.

Chapter 4: HISTORICAL OVERVIEW

The historical overview of Copa America gives a fascinating peek into the growth of South American football and the lasting influence of the competition. From its modest origins in 1916 to its prominence as one of the most important championships in world football, the Copa Copa America has been a symbol of excellence, passion, and unity for generations of players and spectators.

Over the years, the event has seen great performances, momentous triumphs, and moments of sheer enchantment on the field. From the supremacy of famous teams like Brazil and Argentina to the advent of new competitors, Copa America has remained a demonstration of ability, talent, and dedication. As the tournament continues to grow and adapt to the shifting dynamics of the global football scene, its rich history stands as a tribute to the lasting ability of the beautiful game to inspire, unite, and transcend boundaries.

Past Winners and Runners-Up

Copa America, the oldest international continental football tournament, features a rich history steeped in tradition, drama, and moments of genius. Since its start in 1916, the event has seen the birth of renowned teams and individuals who have left an everlasting imprint on the sport. Here's a detailed look at the previous champions and runners-up of Copa America, displaying the successes and heartbreaks that have characterized the event throughout the years:

ARGENTINA:
Winners: 1921, 1925, 1927, 1929, 1937, 1941, 1945, 1946, 1947, 1955, 1957, 1959, 1991, 1993, 2021
Runners-Up: 1916, 1917, 1920, 1923, 1924, 1926, 1935, 1939, 1942, 1959, 1967, 2004, 2007, 2015, 2016

URUGUAY:
Winners: 1916, 1917, 1920, 1923, 1924, 1926, 1935, 1942, 1956, 1959, 1967, 1983, 1987,1995, 1995, and 2011.
Runners-Up: 1919, 1922, 1928, 1939, 1941, 1946, 1957, 1959, 1967, 1975, 1989, 1999, 2004, 2007, 2019

BRAZIL:
Winners: 1919, 1922, 1922, 1949, 1989, 1997, 1999, 2004, 2007, 2019
Runners-Up: 1921, 1925, 1937, 1945, 1946, 1953, 1957, 1959, 1983, 1991, 1995, 2001, 2004, 2007

CHILE:
Winners: 2015, 2016
Runners-Up: 1955, 1956, 1979, 1987, 2015

PARAGUAY:
Winners: 1953, 1979
Runners-up: 1922, 1929, 1947, 1963, 2011

PERU:
Winners: 1939, 1975
Runners-Up: 1935

VENEZUELA:
Winners: None
Runners-Up: 1967

BOLIVIA:
Winners: 1963
Runners-Up: 1997

MEXICO:
Winners: 1993, 2001
Runners-up: 1993, 2001

COLOMBIA:
Winners: 2001
Runners-up: 1975, 1993

COSTA RICA:
Winners: None
Runners-Up: 2003

ECUADOR:
Winners: None
Runners-Up: 1959

UNITED STATES:
Winners: None
Runners-up: 1993, 2016

The list of former champions and runners-up of Copa America highlights the dynamic and competitive spirit of South American football. From regular competitors like Argentina and Uruguay to surprise champions like Chile and Colombia, each country has contributed to the rich fabric of footballing history in the event. As

Copa America continues to expand and attract fans across the globe, the legacy of former winners and runners-up serves as a reminder of the passion, talent, and eternal spirit of the beautiful game.

Memorable Moments in Copa America History

Copa America, entrenched in a century-long history, has generated countless remarkable events that have carved themselves into the annals of footballing tradition. From surprising shocks to amazing goals, these moments have captivated fans and made a lasting mark on the tournament's heritage. Here are some of the most amazing moments in Copa America'sAmerica's history:

MARACANAZO (1950): Uruguay's surprise win against Brazil in the final of the 1950 Copa America, widely known as the "Maracanazo," remains one of the biggest shocks in football history. Against all odds, Uruguay overcame the host nation, Brazil, Brazil, 2-1 at the Maracanã Stadium in Rio de Janeiro, silencing the home fans and capturing their second Copa America championship.

ARGENTINA'S DOMINANCE (1940s–1950s1940s–1950s): During the 1940s and 1950s, Argentina established itself as a dominating force in Copa America, winning the event on many occasions. Led by famous players such as Alfredo Di Stefano and

Omar Sivori, Argentina exhibited talent, flair, and tactical genius, making a lasting impression on the tournament.

CHILE'S BACK-TO-BACK TITLES (2015, 2016):

Chile's back-to-back victory in the 2015 and 2016 editions of Copa America signified a historic milestone for the country. Under the tutelage of coach Jorge Sampaoli and with star players like Alexis Sanchez and Arturo Vidal, Chile exhibited an exciting style of football en route to successive championships, solidifying their place as a strong power in South American football.

MESSI'S MAGICAL MOMENTS: Lionel Messi, generally considered one of the best players of all time, has graced Copa America with countless spectacular moments. From breathtaking dribbles to amazing goals, Messi's exploits have thrilled spectators and shown his enormous brilliance on the continental stage, despite Argentina's elusive pursuit of a Copa America victory over his career.

BRAZIL'S HISTORIC 9-0 VICTORY (1949): In the 1949 edition of Copa America, Brazil recorded a historic 9-0 victory against Ecuador, a result that remains the highest margin of victory in the tournament's history. The match demonstrated Brazil's offensive brilliance and emphasized the nation's supremacy in South American football during that period.

COLOMBIA'S SPECTACULAR JOURNEY (2001): In the 2001 Copa America, Colombia went on a spectacular journey to the title, defeating Mexico in the final to capture their first and only Copa America victory. Led by coach Francisco Maturana and featuring exceptional performances from players like Ivan Cordoba and Victor Aristizabal, Colombia's win symbolized the nation's football revival.

PERU'S FAIRYTALE TRIP (2019): In the 2019 Copa America, Peru won the hearts of football fans with their fairytale trip to the final. Despite being considered underdogs, Peru upset traditional powerhouses Uruguay and Chile on the way to the final, where they eventually succumbed to Brazil. Nevertheless, Peru's passionate efforts and surprising win created a memorable tale for the tournament.

These notable moments in Copa America's history serve as a monument to the tournament's long heritage and the emotion, drama, and excitement that characterize South American football. As supporters anxiously await future editions of Copa America, they do so intending to see more amazing events that will be inscribed into footballing mythology for centuries to come.

Chapter 5: PLAYER RECORDS

Player records in Copa America history serve as a monument to the unique brilliance and lasting skill shown by players in the continental arena. From prolific goal scorers to creative playmakers, these records reflect the outstanding talent and influence of individuals who have made an everlasting imprint on the event. As fans remember prior editions of Copa America, they recall the great performances and extraordinary accomplishments performed by players who have engraved their names into footballing history.

Whether it's the awe-inspiring goal-scoring exploits of great strikers or the precise assists supplied by creative midfielders, player records in Copa America serve as a source of inspiration and respect for football aficionados throughout the globe. As the event continues to change and new players emerge, these records serve as a tribute to the long tradition of Copa America and the eternal brilliance of its top performances.

Highest Goal Scorers

Here are the twenty top goal scorers in Copa America history, history, along with the amount of goals they have scored:

Player	Country	Goals
Norberto Méndez	Argentina	17
Zizinho	Brazil	17
Severino Varela	Uruguay	15
Lolo Fernández	Peru	15
Eduardo Vargas	Chile	14
Paolo Guerrero	Peru	14
Ademir	Brazil	13
Jair	Brazil	13
Lionel Messi	Argentina	13
Gabriel Batistuta	Argentina	13
Héctor Scarone	Uruguay	13
Jóse Manuel Moreno	Argentina	13

Roberto Porta	Uruguay	12
Ángel Romano	Uruguay	12
Didi	Brazil	11
Herminio Masantonio	Argentina	11
Ronaldo	Brazil	10
Arnoldo Iguarán	Colombia	10
Enrique Hormazábal	Chile	10
Ángel Labruna	Argentina	10
Javier Ambrois	Uruguay	10
Pedro Petrone	Uruguay	10
Héctor Castro	Uruguay	10
Óscar Gómez Sánchez	Peru	10

These players have made a lasting mark on Copa America history with their goal-scoring prowess, earning their position as legends of the event.

Players With the Most Assists

Here are the players with the most assists in Copa America history, along with the amount of assists they have recorded:

Player	Country	Assists
Lionel Messi	Argentina	14
Neymar	Brazil	12
Javier Zanetti	Argentina	11
Roberto Dinamite	Brazil	10
Juan Román Riquelme	Argentina	10
Ronaldinho	Brazil	9
Ricardo Bochini	Argentina	8
Diego Maradona	Argentina	8
Carlos Tevez	Argentina	8
Alexis Sánchez	Chile	7
Claudio López	Argentina	7
Daniel Passarella	Argentina	7
Gonzalo Higuaín	Argentina	7
Diego Forlán	Uruguay	7

Cafu	Brazil	7
José Manuel Moreno	Argentina	7
Zico	Brazil	6
Ronald Koeman	Netherlands	6
Marcelo Salas	Chile	6
Juan Arango	Venezuela	6
Hugo Sánchez	Mexico	6
Raúl Vicente Amarilla	Paraguay	6
Roberto Carlos	Brazil	6
Mario Kempes	Argentina	6
Alexis Sánchez	Chile	6
Arturo Vidal	Chile	6

These players have demonstrated their excellent vision and playmaking ability by producing multiple assists during their Copa America careers, contributing greatly to their teams' success in the event.

Chapter 6: KEY STATISTICS AND MILESTONES

Key statistics and events in Copa America history give a fascinating glimpse into the tournament's progress and effect on the world of football. From record-breaking goal-scoring heroics to astonishing performances by players of all ages, these statistics and milestones reveal the tournament's complex tapestry of wins and moments of glory. As fans reminisce on prior editions of Copa America, they marvel at the amazing skill and tenacity demonstrated by individuals and teams alike. Whether it's the youngest prodigies making their mark on the international scene or seasoned veterans overcoming age to play at the greatest level, Copa America is a showcase of the myriad skills and tales that characterize football's lasting allure.

As the tournament continues to captivate the hearts and minds of millions of fans across the world, these major statistics and milestones serve as a tribute to the event's status as a cornerstone of South American football and a celebration of the beautiful game in all its grandeur.

Most Goals Scored in a Single Tournament

The record for the most goals scored by a single player in a Copa America tournament remains a monument to individual brilliance and remarkable skill on the continental level. Throughout the tournament's rich history, some players have left an unforgettable impact by demonstrating their goal-scoring abilities and helping their teams to triumph. From legendary strikers to budding stars, these players have captivated fans with their talent, tenacity, and ability to reach the back of the goal with amazing regularity.

One of the most astounding feats in Copa America history occurred in the 1949 edition of the tournament, when Norberto "Tucho" Méndez, an Argentine striker, carved his name into the record books by scoring an incredible 17 goals in a single tournament. Méndez's amazing goal-scoring run powered Argentina to their seventh Copa America victory and confirmed his place as one of the finest players of his age.

Born on December 12, 1923, in Avellaneda, Argentina, Norberto Méndez came to notoriety as a prolific goal scorer for both club and nation. Known for his speed, agility, and precise finishing, Méndez had a brilliant career that saw him represent teams like Independiente, Racing Club, and Rosario Central, as well as the Argentine national team.

Méndez's remarkable performance in the 1949 Copa America competition proved his ability to rise to the occasion on the highest platform. Throughout the tournament, he displayed his aptitude for finding space in the opposition's defense, his deadly finishing ability, and his capability to produce when it counted most. Whether via well-timed runs, accurate headers, or clinical strikes from distance, Méndez left a path of defenders in his wake and carved his name into footballing mythology with each goal he scored.

One of Méndez's most noteworthy performances occurred in Argentina's first match of the tournament against Ecuador. In a spectacular show of offensive brilliance, Méndez scored an astounding six goals as Argentina cruised to a stunning 12-0 win. His amazing performance not only set the tone for Argentina's campaign but also served as a warning to its competitors of the danger presented by Méndez.

As the competition proceeded, Méndez continued to terrorize opposition defenders with his dangerous mix of speed, skill, and goal-scoring instinct. Whether playing major footballing countries or lesser-known opponents, Méndez remained a consistent danger, always ready to grasp the opportunity and produce for his side.

In the final match of the tournament against Brazil, Méndez once again rose to the occasion, scoring a critical goal to assist Argentina earn a hard-fought 2-2 draw and claim the Copa America championship. His goal-scoring exploits throughout the tournament garnered him global accolades and cemented him as one of the finest performers in Copa America history.

Norberto Méndez's record-breaking performance in the 1949 Copa America tournament serves as a monument to his outstanding skill, perseverance, and ability to flourish under duress. His 17 goals in a single tournament remain a standard of greatness and serve as a reminder of the lasting influence that individual brilliance may have on the result of a tournament.

Norberto "Tucho" Méndez's record for the most goals scored in a single Copa America tournament is a testimonial to his great skill and goal-scoring ability. His extraordinary success in the 1949 edition of the tournament highlighted his ability to rise to the occasion on the largest platform and confirmed his place as one of the finest players in Copa America history. As fans continue to marvel at his amazing performance, Méndez's legacy serves as a source of motivation for future generations of players aiming to make their imprint on the continental arena.

Youngest and Oldest Players to Participate

In the Copa America history, the competition has seen the involvement of players from diverse age groups, ranging from youthful prodigies to seasoned veterans. These players have exhibited their skill and perseverance on the continental stage, making an everlasting stamp on the tournament's heritage. Among them, the youngest and oldest players to ever compete in the Copa America retain a particular position in football legend.

The youngest player to ever grace the Copa America stage is Juan Errazquin, who represented Uruguay at the early age of 15 years and 9 months. Errazquin made his debut in the 1916 edition of the event, demonstrating his precocious skill and earning a place in history as the youngest player to compete in the Copa America. Despite his youth, Errazquin's participation in the Uruguay team spoke much about his extraordinary skill and future as a player.

On the opposite end of the scale, the oldest player to appear in the Copa America is Zizinho, the Brazilian football hero who represented his nation at the age of 41 years and 9 months. Zizinho, famous for his talent, vision, and originality on the field, made his last Copa America participation in the 1957 edition of the tournament, displaying his continuing enthusiasm for the game and his amazing longevity as a player.

These two players, Juan Errazquin and Zizinho symbolize the extremes of age in Copa America's history, showcasing the tournament's capacity to draw talent from all eras. From the young enthusiasm of Errazquin to the seasoned wisdom of Zizinho, their contributions to the event serve as a monument to the worldwide appeal and long legacy of Copa America.

Record Attendance and Television Viewership

Copa America, being one of the most renowned football competitions in the world, has garnered large crowds and broadcast coverage throughout its history. The tournament's record attendance and broadcast viewing records serve as a tribute to its great popularity and ongoing appeal among football fans worldwide.

One of the most noteworthy instances of record attendance in Copa America history came during the 1949 tournament hosted in Brazil. The final match between Brazil and Paraguay played at the Maracanã Stadium in Rio de Janeiro, gathered an incredible audience of over 170,000 people, making it the biggest attendance ever recorded for a Copa America contest. The explosive atmosphere and enthusiastic support from the spectators produced a remarkable spectacle that stays carved in the memory of football lovers.

In terms of television viewership, Copa America has routinely drawn millions of fans from across the world, eager to watch the drama, excitement, and talent on exhibit in each match. While particular data may fluctuate from year to year, the tournament's broadcast reach stretches to various nations across multiple continents, assuring comprehensive coverage and accessibility for fans worldwide.

One significant example of record television viewership came during the 2019 Copa America event hosted in Brazil. The final match between Brazil and Peru, aired to audiences worldwide, drew an estimated television viewership of over 50 million people, making it one of the most-watched athletic events of the year. The tough competition, huge stakes, and star-studded list of players captivated the interest of spectators, leading to the tournament's overall success and popularity.

These unprecedented attendance and broadcast viewing numbers emphasize the worldwide popularity and relevance of Copa America as a major football championship. As the event continues to expand and fascinate fans with its exciting matches and memorable moments, it remains a beacon of excellence and a celebration of the beautiful game in the world arena.

Chapter 7: COPA AMERICA 2024 PREDICTIONS

As the this event approaches, expectation increases for an explosive competition featuring the finest of South American football. With a long history of strong rivalry and spectacular events, fans anxiously anticipate the drama and excitement that lie ahead. As teams prepare to vie for continental glory, speculation runs wild about likely results and noteworthy players. Amidst the excitement, one thing is certain: the scene is set for a dramatic show of talent, emotion, and resolve. With each match ready to bring twists, turns, and moments of brilliance, Copa America 2024 promises to be a tournament to remember. As fans across the globe gear up to cheer on their favorite teams and players, the scene is prepared for football brilliance to take center stage once again.

Favorites for Winning the Tournament

The enthusiasm and expectation surrounding the event are apparent. Football fans across the globe anxiously anticipate the battle of titans as South America's top teams compete for continental dominance. While forecasting the result of such a renowned competition is intrinsically tough, certain clubs stand out as favorites to take the prized trophy based on their current play, squad depth, and previous success.

ARGENTINA: With a long history in Copa America, including 15 victories, Argentina begins the tournament as one of the frontrunners for success. Led by the great Lionel Messi, who continues to defy age with his exceptional skill and leadership, Argentina features a superb roster capable of crushing any opponent. Supported by a solid supporting cast comprising players like Paulo Dybala, Lautaro Martinez, and Rodrigo De Paul, Argentina boasts the firepower and experience required to go all the way in Copa America 2024.

BRAZIL: As the reigning champions and the most successful team in Copa America history with nine championships, Brazil always looms big as a difficult opponent. Despite suffering hurdles in previous editions of the competition, Brazil remains a force to be reckoned with, with a plethora of quality across every position. Spearheaded by the likes of Neymar, Casemiro, and Richarlison, Brazil's offensive brilliance and defensive stability make them great challengers to maintain their championship and add another chapter to their famous Copa America record.

URUGUAY: With 15 Copa America championships to their record, Uruguay is another consistent force in South American football. Known for their toughness, perseverance, and tactical astuteness, Uruguay constantly presents a danger in big events. Led by seasoned stalwarts such as Luis Suarez and Edinson Cavani,

Uruguay mixes defensive stability with precision finishing to frustrate opponents and grind out victories. Despite their aged lineup, Uruguay's depth of experience and winning mindset make them a formidable challenge for any side in the Copa America 2024.

COLOMBIA: While Colombia has yet to win a Copa America championship, they routinely play well and are considered dark horses for the event. With a combination of technical brilliance, physicality, and tactical flexibility, Colombia boasts the skills to compete with the best. Led by James Rodriguez and Juan Cuadrado, Colombia's offensive flair and inventiveness represent a continuous danger to opposition defenders. With a quality group eager for victory, Colombia might surprise many and create a real bid for the Copa America championship.

CHILE: Despite their relatively modest size, Chile has developed as a force to be reckoned with in South American football in recent years. With back-to-back Copa America victories in 2015 and 2016, Chile has demonstrated its capacity to compete with the continent's finest. While their golden generation may be older, Chile still possesses a superb roster including the likes of Alexis Sanchez and Arturo Vidal. Known for their high-intensity pressing and offensive football, Chile's unrelenting approach might see them make a deep run in the Copa America 2024.

POTENTIAL CONTENDERS: Other teams like Peru, Ecuador, and Paraguay cannot be disregarded, as they feature excellent squads capable of creating shocks and disturbing the preparations of the favorites. Peru, in particular, has demonstrated perseverance and drive in previous editions of the Copa America, reaching the final in 2019. Ecuador, with their young zeal and attacking flair, might surprise many with their performances. Meanwhile, Paraguay's defensive stability and tactical discipline make them a formidable opponent for any side.

As the day draws nearer, viewers can anticipate a fascinating event packed with drama, excitement, and moments of genius. While favorites may develop, the unpredictable nature of football assures that anything may happen on the way to triumph. With the attention of the footballing world locked on South America, the scene is set for another spectacular edition of Copa America.

Top Candidates for the Golden Boot and Golden Glove Awards

In every big football event like Copa America, the race for individual honors such as the Golden Boot and Golden Glove is as eagerly awaited as the chase for the trophy itself. While predicting the winners of these prizes is intrinsically hard, certain players stand out as major candidates based on their prior results, present form, and likely effect on the event.

Golden Boot Contenders:

LIONEL MESSI (ARGENTINA): Widely recognized as one of the best players of all time, Lionel Messi is consistently a contender for the Golden Boot. With his outstanding goal-scoring ability, vision, and inventiveness, Messi has the potential to dominate the competition and top the scoring charts.

NEYMAR (BRAZIL): As the talismanic figure for the reigning champs, Neymar has the talent and flair to light up Copa America. Known for his dribbling abilities, precision finishing, and ability to create opportunities, Neymar is a strong candidate to win the Golden Boot.

LAUTARO MARTINEZ (ARGENTINA): With his deadly finishing and savvy movement off the ball, Lautaro Martinez has established himself as one of the most promising young attackers in international football. If he maintains his current form, Martinez might emerge as a surprise candidate for the Golden Boot.

LUIS SUAREZ (URUGUAY): A seasoned goal-scorer with a flair for hitting the back of the net, Luis Suarez provides a continuous danger to opposition defenders. With his size, talent, and predatory instincts, Suarez is a great possibility to lead Uruguay's attack and fight for the Golden Boot.

ALEXIS SANCHEZ (CHILE): Despite his increasing age, Alexis Sanchez remains a potent goal-scoring threat for Chile. With his mobility, dribbling skill, and accurate finishing, Sanchez has the potential to make a huge impact and contend for the Golden Boot.

Golden Glove Contenders:

ALISSON BECKER (BRAZIL): As one of the finest goalkeepers in the world, Alisson Becker is a major candidate for the Golden Glove. Known for his shot-stopping skills, authoritative presence, and great distribution, Alisson might play a significant part in Brazil's defense.

EMILIANO MARTINEZ (ARGENTINA): After his great performances for Argentina in previous competitions, Emiliano Martinez has established himself as a trustworthy last line of defense. With his shot-stopping skills, coolness under pressure, and leadership abilities, Martinez is a good contender for the Golden Glove.

DAVID OSPINA (COLOMBIA): Experienced and trustworthy, David Ospina has been a constant in Colombia's goal for many years. With his agility, reflexes, and organizational abilities, Ospina is a strong force between the posts and a candidate for the Golden Glove.

KEYLOR NAVAS (COSTA RICA): A senior goalkeeper with a plethora of experience at the top level, Keylor Navas is recognized for his acrobatic saves and ability to come up big on important occasions. As Costa Rica's uncontested number one, Navas is a strong prospect for the Golden Glove.

PEDRO GALLESE (PERU): With his athleticism, agility, and shot-stopping abilities, Pedro Gallese has established himself as one of the greatest goalkeepers in South America. As Peru's final line of defense, Gallese might make a huge impact and challenge for the Golden Glove.

While these players are among the leading candidates for the Golden Boot and Golden Glove honors, Copa America is notorious for generating surprising heroes and exceptional performances. As the tournament develops, viewers can anticipate entertaining matches and unforgettable moments as the race for individual awards heats up alongside the struggle for continental triumph.

Potential Upsets and Surprises

In any football tournament, there's always the opportunity for shocks and surprises that capture spectators and defy expectations. Copa America 2024 is no exception, with numerous teams prepared to spice up the competition and challenge the traditional favorites. While forecasting individual surprises is intrinsically impossible, various variables might lead to surprising outcomes and dramatic narratives throughout the game.

One possible source of shocks is the development of excellent young players from lesser-known footballing countries. Countries like Ecuador, Venezuela, and Peru have increasingly produced outstanding young players who have made huge contributions to the international arena. With their desire, bravery, and technical talent, these players might lead their teams to surprising triumphs and disrupt the tournament's established order.

The limited timetable and rigorous nature of international competitions may lead to unforeseen results. Fatigue, injuries, and tactical tweaks may all play a part in molding the course of the tournament and offering possibilities for underdog teams to overcome the odds and achieve victory.

In addition to that, the Copa America structure, which involves a combination of round-robin group matches followed by knockout rounds, gives abundant potential for unexpected outcomes and Cinderella tales. A single moment of brilliance, a well-executed game plan or a stroke of luck may shift the tide in favor of the underdog and shock the tournament favorites.

Historically, Copa America has been host to countless shocks and surprises that have caught the imagination of football fans throughout the globe. Whether it's a plucky underdog beating the odds to shock a heavyweight contender or a budding star declaring their presence on the world scene, the event is packed with opportunities for unexpected twists and turns.

As Copa America 2024 unfolds, spectators may anticipate the unexpected as teams strive for glory and domination on the continental stage. While the favorites may dominate the headlines, it's frequently the underdogs and dark horses who give the most memorable moments and enduring effects. With passion, talent, and drive on show, Copa America is guaranteed to produce its fair share of shocks and surprises that will have viewers on the edge of their seats until the final whistle blows.

Chapter 8: SOCIAL AND CULTURAL INFLUENCE

Copa America's social and cultural significance reaches well beyond the football surface, affecting the identity and collective consciousness of South American countries. The event acts as a uniting factor, bringing together disparate populations and developing a feeling of national pride and solidarity. From the streets to the stadiums, Copa America generates passion and excitement among supporters of all ages and backgrounds, overcoming socio-economic boundaries and encouraging inclusion.

Beyond its sports importance, Copa America serves as a platform for honoring the rich cultural legacy of South America, displaying music, dance, and food that represent the region's colorful variety. Through its power to inspire, unify, and celebrate, Copa America has an enduring legacy that continues beyond the final whistle, enhancing the social fabric and cultural tapestry of the continent.

Influence of Copa America on South American Culture

Copa America, South America's biggest football competition, occupies a particular place in the hearts and thoughts of millions throughout the continent. Beyond the field of athletics, Copa America has a deep impact on South American culture, molding social standards, promoting national identity, and uniting various groups in a common celebration of football brilliance.

At its heart, Copa America is more than simply a football event; it is a reflection of South America's rich cultural legacy and collective enthusiasm for the beautiful game. From the busy streets of Buenos Aires to the sun-drenched beaches of Rio de Janeiro, the event serves as a focal point for communities to join together and enjoy the pleasure and thrill of football. In every part of the continent, Copa America sparks a feeling of pride and solidarity, transcending geographical borders and establishing a common sense of identity among South Americans.

One of the most prominent ways in which Copa America impacts South American culture is via its celebration of national pride and patriotism. As teams from around the continent battle for success on the field, supporters gather behind their own countries, decorating themselves in national colors, waving flags, and screaming anthems in support of their teams. This outpouring of national pride provides a real feeling of brotherhood and unity among supporters, underscoring the primacy of national identity in South American society.

Furthermore, Copa America provides a showcase for the distinct cultural traditions and customs of each participant country. Whether it's the samba rhythms of Brazil, the tango melodies of Argentina, or the cumbia beats of Colombia, the competition gives a platform for South American nations to express their cultural heritage via music, dance, and food. This cultural exchange creates a greater awareness and knowledge of the different cultures that make up the fabric of South America, encouraging cross-cultural conversation and mutual respect across countries.

Also, Copa America has a huge influence on the cultural environment of South American towns and communities. As host towns prepare to welcome teams and supporters from across the globe, they undergo a makeover, with streets decked with banners and decorations, stadiums vibrating with energy and enthusiasm, and local businesses bustling with activity. This inflow of tourists not only benefits the local economy but also produces a dynamic environment of friendliness and kindness, exhibiting the finest that South American culture has to offer to the globe.

In addition to its cultural importance, Copa America has a crucial role in establishing the communal memory and identity of South American countries. Iconic incidents from earlier tournaments, such as Maracanazo, Brazil's supremacy in the 1970s, and Argentina's wins under Diego Maradona, are engraved into the collective memory of football fans throughout the continent, acting as touchstones of national pride and sports performance.

Overall, the effect of Copa America on South American culture is significant and far-reaching, influencing every part of life, from sports and entertainment to politics and identity. As the event continues to grow and fascinate fans with its exciting matches and memorable moments, its cultural heritage will persist, providing a tribute to the everlasting power of football to connect and inspire people across borders and generations.

Economic and Tourism Impact of Hosting the Tournament

The economic and tourist benefits of hosting the Copa America event are enormous, giving host nations a chance to display their hospitality, infrastructure, and cultural legacy to the globe while driving economic growth and development.

Hosting the Copa America generates a flood of people from across the world, including football fans, media workers, and dignitaries, leading to increased tourist income for the host country. Hotels, restaurants, bars, and local businesses witness an increase in patronage as tourists swarm to the host towns, earning revenue and providing employment possibilities for inhabitants. Additionally, the flood of visitors boosts demand for different products and services, resulting in increased consumer spending and economic activity in the host nation.

Hosting the Copa America gives host towns a chance to display their infrastructure and services on a worldwide platform.

Stadiums, transportation networks, hotels, and other important facilities undergo repairs and renovations in preparation for the event, providing a lasting legacy of better infrastructure for local inhabitants and tourists alike. These expenditures not only strengthen the host city's potential to host significant events in the future but also help long-term economic growth and urban redevelopment initiatives.

Furthermore, hosting the Copa America boosts the host country's worldwide image and reputation, garnering attention from visitors, investors, and possible commercial partners. The event acts as a platform for showcasing the host nation's cultural legacy, natural beauty, and tourism attractions, attracting tourists to see the country beyond the bounds of the football surface. This enhanced exposure helps to present the host country as an attractive location for tourism, commerce, and investment, creating international relationships and collaborations that benefit the local economy.

In addition to the direct economic effect, hosting the Copa America provides intangible advantages for the host country, including the development of national pride, solidarity, and social cohesion. The event draws people together from varied origins and cultures, generating a feeling of brotherhood and unity among spectators and locals alike. This feeling of communal spirit and common purpose transcends boundaries and obstacles, presenting a favorable image of the host country on the world stage.

It is vital to remember that hosting large athletic events like the Copa America also carries expenses and hazards for host nations. Investments in infrastructure and security may be expensive, and there is always the possibility of logistical issues, security concerns, and economic disruptions. Therefore, thorough preparation, coordination, and risk management are required to guarantee that the advantages of hosting the tournament surpass the expenses and that the event leaves a good and enduring legacy for the host country and its people.

The economic and tourist effect of hosting the Copa America is multidimensional, comprising both real and intangible advantages for the host nation. By exploiting the tournament as a platform to exhibit their culture, infrastructure, and hospitality, host nations may enjoy the fruits of increased tourism, investment, and worldwide recognition while encouraging national pride, solidarity, and social cohesion among their inhabitants.

Social Initiatives and Community Engagement

Social initiatives and community participation play a key role in the Copa America competition, developing a feeling of duty and solidarity among participating countries while having a beneficial influence on local communities.

One of the key social projects related to Copa America is the promotion of inclusiveness and diversity within the football community. The competition provides a platform for promoting the varied cultures, identities, and origins of South American countries, developing mutual respect and understanding among players, spectators, and stakeholders. Initiatives such as anti-discrimination campaigns, diversity seminars, and inclusive fan engagement initiatives strive to fight prejudice and foster a culture of acceptance and tolerance within the football community.

Additionally, Copa America offers a chance for social engagement and community development activities aiming at addressing important social concerns and fostering positive change. Through cooperation with local NGOs, charities, and grassroots groups, the tournament organizers conduct different community-based initiatives centered on education, health, environmental sustainability, and youth empowerment. These projects strive to harness the power of football as a force for social good, utilizing the tournament's platform to make lasting effects and better the lives of disadvantaged and neglected people.

Copa America supports environmental sustainability and eco-consciousness via different green projects and eco-friendly activities. From trash reduction and recycling schemes to carbon offsetting measures and renewable energy solutions, the event administrators stress environmental responsibility and attempt to limit the tournament's ecological imprint. By increasing awareness about environmental challenges and supporting sustainable practices, Copa America strives to inspire positive change and urge fans and stakeholders to embrace more ecologically friendly lives.

Copa America supports community involvement and participation via grassroots football programs, youth development projects, and sports diplomacy activities. These projects seek to strengthen local communities, promote social inclusion, and give chances for impoverished youngsters to engage in structured sports and leisure activities. By utilizing the power of football as a tool for social change, Copa America aspires to establish a legacy of inspiration, opportunity, and hope for future generations.

Social activities and community participation are fundamental components of the Copa America competition, indicating its dedication to utilizing football as a catalyst for good social change. By fostering inclusion, diversity, environmental sustainability, and community development, Copa America strives to create a lasting legacy of empowerment, togetherness, and solidarity that goes beyond the borders of the football field. Through joint efforts and collective action, Copa America strives to use the worldwide appeal of football to solve social concerns, promote social justice, and create a more equal and inclusive society for everyone.

Chapter 9: ANTICIPATION AND EXPECTATIONS

The anticipation and expectations surrounding Copa America 2024 are at an all-time high as football fans excitedly anticipate the commencement of South America's greatest international event. With a rich history, strong rivalry, and a record of delivering unforgettable moments, Copa America aims to produce another spectacular edition that captivates spectators across the globe.

As the tournament approaches, excitement mounts for the battle of Titans as South America's top teams fight for continental dominance. With perennial powerhouses like Argentina, Brazil, and Uruguay leading the charge, expectations are high for passionate clashes, dramatic shocks, and legendary performances on the field. The thought of watching footballing giants such as Lionel Messi, Neymar, and Luis Suarez in action adds to the anticipation, as supporters anxiously await the chance to see their favorite players flourish on the international stage.

Moreover, Copa America 2024 carries unique importance as it represents the tournament's return to the United States, a nation with a rising love for football and a diversified population that embraces the sport with enthusiasm. The choice to hold the event in the U.S. highlights the expanding worldwide popularity of Copa America and underlines the sport's capacity to transcend geographical barriers and unify supporters from all countries and backgrounds.

Copa America 2024 arrives at a period of increased confidence and enthusiasm for the future of South American football. With a new generation of brilliant players rising throughout the continent, there is a feeling of anticipation about the possibility for fresh faces to make their mark and display their abilities on the world stage. From budding talents like Vinicius Junior and Erling Haaland to established veterans wanting one final chance at success, the event gives a platform for players to create their chapter in football history.

Furthermore, Copa America 2024 gives a chance for host towns to demonstrate their hospitality, infrastructure, and cultural history to the globe while driving economic growth and development. The tournament's influence goes beyond the football ground, offering a boost to local companies, tourism, and job creation, and leaving a lasting legacy of enhanced infrastructure and a worldwide reputation for the host country.

Overall, the anticipation and expectations for Copa America 2024 are sky-high as supporters anxiously anticipate the start of the tournament and the chance to experience the drama, excitement, and emotion that characterize South American football. With a roster of powerful teams, burgeoning talent, and the background of the United States, Copa America 2024 promises to be a spectacle that catches the imagination and makes a lasting impact on football fans across the globe.

Legacy and Significance of the Tournament in Football History

The importance and significance of Copa America in football history are significant, molding the character of South American football and leaving an everlasting effect on the global sports scene. As the oldest international football event in the world, Copa America retains a particular place in the hearts of football fans, signifying a celebration of the beautiful game and the rich cultural history of South America.

One of the most lasting legacies of the Copa America is its role in raising South American football to worldwide prominence. Since its establishment in 1916, the event has served as a showcase for the continent's greatest footballing talent, offering a platform for famous players such as Pele, Diego Maradona, and Lionel Messi to amaze viewers with their ability, inventiveness, and enthusiasm for the game. The tournament's historic history is packed with memorable moments and amazing matches that have enthralled generations of football fans and solidified South America's status as a hub of football brilliance.

Moreover, Copa America has played a crucial role in defining the growth of international football and the internationalization of the sport. As one of the oldest and most famous international events, Copa America has inspired the formation of comparable contests across the globe, including the UEFA European

Championship, the Africa Cup of Nations, and the CONCACAF Gold Cup. The tournament's significance extends well beyond South America, serving as a model for worldwide football governance, competitive organization, and commercial growth.

Copa America has been a catalyst for social development and togetherness throughout South America, developing a feeling of national pride, identity, and solidarity among participant countries. The event serves as a strong symbol of togetherness and collaboration, bringing together many cultures, languages, and traditions in a common celebration of football brilliance. Through its capacity to transcend boundaries and connect individuals from various origins, Copa America encourages mutual respect, understanding, and goodwill among countries, helping to regional stability and peace.

The game has had a substantial economic influence on host nations, promoting tourism, infrastructure development, and job creation while earning cash for local companies and communities. The tournament's capacity to draw people from across the globe and highlight the host country's culture, hospitality, and facilities has led to its standing as a significant athletic event with far-reaching economic advantages.

The importance and significance of Copa America in football history are unequaled, marking a tribute to the continuing ability of the beautiful game to inspire, unify, and alter lives. As South America's greatest international football event, Copa America continues to fascinate fans with its rich history, strong competition, and memorable moments, cementing its position as a treasured institution in the global footballing scene for centuries to come.

CONCLUSION

The Copa America stands as a beacon of excellence and a celebration of the beautiful game, leaving an unforgettable impact on football history and the hearts of fans worldwide. With its rich heritage, historic past, and ongoing relevance, Copa America symbolizes the summit of South American football and a display of the continent's footballing prowess, cultural variety, and sports enthusiasm.

Throughout its historic history, Copa America has served as a venue for memorable moments, renowned players, and spectacular matches that have captivated generations of football lovers and generated a strong feeling of national pride and solidarity among participant countries. From the magnificent goals of Maradona and Messi to the tactical genius of Brazil and Uruguay, the tournament has generated innumerable moments that will be enjoyed for years to come.

Its effect goes beyond the football ground, affecting the evolution of international football, encouraging social cohesion and togetherness within South America, and stimulating economic growth and development in host nations. As a symbol of greatness, solidarity, and sports triumph, Copa America reflects the global principles of collaboration, dedication, and fair play that transcend boundaries and connect people from all walks of life.

As we look out to the future, Copa America remains a light of hope and inspiration, continuing to inspire generations of players, fans, and countries to aspire for greatness and embrace the spirit of competition, fraternity, and respect. With each edition, the event maintains its status as a cornerstone of football history and a monument to the eternal power of the beautiful game to unite, inspire, and alter lives.

In the annals of football history, Copa America stands tall as a tribute to the lasting ability of sport to transcend borders, bridge differences, and bring people together in celebration of shared passion and achievement. As we celebrate its past and look forward to the next chapter in its historic history, Copa America remains a symbol of optimism, togetherness, and the global language of football that continues to inspire and connect us all.

Printed in Great Britain
by Amazon

42871031R00044